Frederick Douglas Boulevard

Poetic Illuminations

Authored By

Frederick Douglas Dixon Jr

Preface

Frederick Douglas Boulevard "Poetic Illuminations" is a collection of my personal life experiences, memories and much more. The adult nature of this book stretches the imagination and some of its works are eloquently explicit in nature. The subject matter and scenarios give you a raw look inside my journey. Some of these experiences go back to the earliest years of my childhood. The pages are filled with real life moments caught in time. The book also contains some of my hopes, aspirations and dreams of what could have been. I have learned throughout my journey to document my thoughts and emotions so profoundly that you can literally feel the passion in my words.

The image on the front cover of this book illustrates the duality of the "Gemini" inside me. The two separate paths represent the paths of "Enlightenment and Spirituality" that I currently travel on. Welcome to my space!

First, I want to give thanks and give praise to my "God" for the blessings that have been provided for me throughout my life. My faith in God allows me to live in a place where positive energy fuels my vibration. This vibration allows me to focus on myself and everything I have created in this world. Thank you, Father God.

Many of the people on my path have helped me a great deal and it would make me proud to acknowledge them in this book.

I would like to give acknowledgement, love and respect to My Grandmother Verna Grinage "Gram" and my Grandfather Clifford Grinage, my "Gramma" Betty "Boo" Garrett, Wallace "Poppo" Peake and My parents Audrey C. Peake, Frederick D. Dixon Sr. and Toni Dixon.

The most important people in my life and my most precious earthly blessings are my four beautiful children. My two beautiful daughters Angeleis Novelle Martinez, Jordan Kristine Dixon and my two son's Santana Tito Dixon and My "Man-Man", Roman Carter Dixon. I love you all so much. Thank you for everything that you are and will be. I am abundantly grateful for all of you. Always, remember you can do anything you put your mind too. I believe that and I believe in you. You got this. Love always, Papi!

As I continue this journey, my cousin and best friend accompanies me. James Rasheim Haslam a.k.a. "BiGG Ra DoGG", I want to thank you for helping me most of all. There were times that life tested me to the limit, and you were right there to help me absorb it all. I cannot express how much you have meant to me, being in my corner all these years. Thank You "Ma Brotha". I hope one day that I can repay the friendship that you have given to me. I strive to be a better man because of you!

I would like to send my love and give a special thank you to my sister Eboney Chaniece Crump and her husband "US Marine Corp Sergeant" Travis Crump, for holding me down while I put my life back together. At the most difficult time in my life, you both sacrificed to help me. I will never forget that and I appreciate you both. Thank You, Ebo, Thank You Travis.

There are so many people that have touch my life, I just want to mention a few more. I want to thank my Stepmother Sandy Trudeau and Richard Trudeau for showing me and my kids' kindness and love throughout my journey. I want to thank Renee Rick, Rosland Rick, Rochelle Ricks, Thomas Porter, Lynn Rick and Robert Ricks for helping to raise me.

I want to send a Shout Out to my brothers and sisters, Corey J Nelson Sr., Ramona Nelson, Eboney Crump, Jahanna Kurtz, Shaquondra Bradley and Wallace Peake Jr.

Shout out to my Auntie's, Nadine Grinage, Marylou Dockstater, Verna Grinage "Auntie Nibbie", Rosland Garrett, Belinda Garrett, Paula Grinage, Constance Grinage "Auntie Connie", Sue Jones, Francis Grinage "Auntie Goo-Goo", Jeanine Grinage, Michelle Boadnax, Annette, Evette and Soupy.

Shout out to my Uncle's, Robert Wayne Grinage "Injun", Carl Doxstater "Rusty", Duane Broadnax, Tony Broadnax, Patrick Garrett and Darnell Garrett.

I want to send my love out to all my nieces and nephews, Reija Brown, Rodney Brown, Amari Mone Lowery and Antoine Lowery Jr., Corey J Nelson Jr. "Kilo", Cadyn Nelson, Monet Harris, Roman Kurtz and most of all Gianna"G.G."Kurtz.

I want to send the biggest shout out to my first cousin and Best Man,"Hell of a Nu" Milton Foster (Nu-Nu) for making sure I graduated High School and looking out for me as a youth, Thanks Nu!

I want to send limitless "Shout Outs" to my hundreds of cousins and other family members that I also want to acknowledge. Tiffany Junior, Asha Jones, Tai Nai Lee Jones, Avi, Stephanie Grinage, Cheryl Marable, Julius Marable, Samila Mathis, Brandy Mathis, Israel "Juice" Douglas, Robert Douglas, Tammy Foster, Jay Anderson, JaiAnna Anderson, Joey D. Huff, Tracy Owens, Tiara Andrew, Cindy Owen, Sabrina Owens, Michael Owens, Marcus Ricks, Jaida, Jaeden, Rell, Shelley, Evan, Lexi, Dawn White, Brandon White, Ra Davis, Yale Davis, Jaqueline Walker, Jackie Walker, Wisdom, Denise Walker, Debbie Danzler, Symore Broadnax, Brandi Broadnax, Damone, Steve Meadows, Mark, Sam, Money Michael

Chisley, Tunita "Cooda" Nelson, Josett Nelson, Ju-Ju, Treasure, Lex, Mikey Dee Dee's, Isaiah Hicklin, Tomisha, Fancy, Correll, Dorelle, Nurelle, Patrick B Garrett Jr. "PJ", Clifford Grinage, Blass, Thomas Hicklin, George Cannon, Noki, Tam, Mannie Fresh, Demarr Dantzler Devaughn Dantzler and a hundred more. One Love Family!

To my "Central Park/Rodney County Fam. Big Up's to Troy Fosset "T-Rock", Kelly Davis, Leo Johnson "Fillmore Leo", Carlos Johnson, Ruben Johnson, Melly Mel, Desmond Brown, Black Ron, Lil Dave, Ms. Mary, Big Dave, Scott Down, White Tony, Wesley, April, Delmar "The Snitch", Freddie Fred Norwood, Big Mia, Bo, The Original JB, Pluke, Jones Bradberry, Sophia-Sophia-Sophia, Coretta, Dre, Ty (The Barber), Marcell "Cell", Donell Gray "D-Nice", Torrey Robinson "T-Rob", Marty Thomas, Glen Johnson, Pooh Wells, Eli Hall, Val, Darren "Huckabee", Duke, Eric Harvey, Mrs. Harvey, Tracy Harvey' Mrs. Johnson, Althia, Kevin White, Lep "Leprechaun", D-Johnson, Jeffrey Williams, Papa D., Da-Da, Prentice and a hundred more. Much love for my Central Park Fam! Shout Out to my classmates and friends at The College of Saint Rose. My Homie "Big Q" a.k.a. "Bobby Digital" Qadir Wilson, Stay Up Big Q. Raul Leon, Danny Martinez, Eric Thomas, Big Pat Filien, Jeff Fryer, Big Earl, Big Chris, "Rob" Ace-Deuce-Trey, Jimmy "The Hat" Fallon, Steve, J. Hartman, Krishna "Harry" Bishop, Shondel Bryant, Danielle, Shalonda, Nika, Anthony Harvey, Big L, Jay, Todd Foster, Rashad, Chris and Corey Carlo, Big Bonzie, Larry Curtis, Ola and Eric Brabham.

The "Mega Shout" goes out to my cousin Dr. Courtney Copeland. You are an aspiration to us all. Congratulations Dr Copeland. You are proof that we can do anything we choose and that hard work pays off. Luv you Cuz.

Special Thanks to: Katherine "Katie" Jean Jung, Crystal Clark, T. Washington, B. Badgett, K. Gonzalez., C. Moore, I. Plaza, G. Tod, B. Streeter, S. Reid, N. Hill, G. Jaramillo, E. Pichardo and D. Stempien.

Lastly, I want to thank everyone who is taking the time to read this book. "Frederick Douglas Blvd" is very personal to me. I feel like I am sharing some of my most intimate thoughts on these pages. I honestly never imagined writing poetry, let alone writing a book of poetry. This is my evolution in literal form, evidently. I never wrote a single word to offend anyone but if I have offended anyone, believe me when I say it, "I meant every word", These are all my experiences.

I am Frederick Douglas Dixon Jr. aka. "Red Man", "Freddy B", "B." and "Red", for anyone unfamiliar. I am half Native American from the "Seneca Nation of Indians" and a Black Man from the eastside of Buffalo, New York.

The origin of my name comes from an American slave named "Frederick Douglass" that ran away from enslavement in the south and gained his freedom in the north. Frederick Douglass then became an abolitionist who fought for the abolishment of slavery, human rights and woman's right.

Peace and Love…

Go Bills!

Contents

Chapter 3 The Poet's Playground

Chapter 4 Introspection

Chapter 5 Slam Poetry

Chapter 1
My Life

Chapter 1 "My Life" describes how infelicitous this journey has been for me. Thankfully, I am still here.

"Life has taught me to count my blessings daily because tomorrow may not get here in time."

-Red Man

Who

Standing on the moon, staring at the sun
Looking at that boy, holding that gun
Will he shoot his future?
Can I save his life?

These are the questions that lurk this night

I must stop that shot, before he drops
I must stand for something, before he becomes nothing

I must not stand quiet
I must not turn away
I must do the right thing
For him to see a better day

I must save that kid
I must stop his plan
I must help that light
He's not yet a man

Will he be that fool that blows his cool?
Or will he be that bold and cut short his goals

I long for that day when he'll find his way
I wish for that night when he sees that light

Until that day I'll always look back
Reminded of me, that kid in fact!

Where I Live

In the neighborhood of dreams
I was fifteen on the block

Ready for the world
With a pocket full of rocks

No one schooled me to the game
No one cares, so why not

All I have is this heart
On a block that's red hot

A stack full of doves
One knot to a pack

A block from the house
So, I can get right back

I am killing myself
Unknowing and in rewind
It was put here to deceive us
As part of his design

The last of the crew
To make water in to wine
I have discovered myself
With a mirror and a rhyme

The flow of a lifetime
Has save me from the hood
With some practice and forgiveness
This life could be pretty good.

Boy 10

A burst of insanity has entered my zone
Massive visions of violence
Right in my home

His knuckles held tight
Her face the blame
Assault on a woman
A man insane

Kicking and screaming
Illuminates the room
A monster of fear
She's scared to move

I've witnessed so much
With few memories of good

Can you imagine this dream?
A nightmare understood!

It's the blessing of life
That I've created this rhyme
Escaping the insanity
That lived in my mind

Seven years of hell
Is what I survived

Two parents not listening
To a young boy's cries!

Run Away

It was a snowy night
It wasn't a dream
He's beating my wisdom
I could hear the screams

I dressed my brother
We were leaving no doubt

I was only five
I could not stay and fight

My brother was three
But I was in charge
As we started to walk
I could hear him cry

Headed to Uncle Bob's
Or so I thought

We were stopped on the street
By a woman in the dark

Where are you going?
She asked us both

We had no answer
We just had to go

We wanted to escape
The violence of that night

We knew nothing of the world
Or dangers in sight

I never thanked that Angel
That saved us from the night
What happened stays with me
Blessed to be alright

The Window

I am 2 years old
Laying under the window
Some one's throwing rocks
I wish it would stop

My mom said don't move
I am trying to be still
My grandma's yelling
You stop; You fool

Glass is falling
There are rocks everywhere
That glass is so noisy
Move, I don't dare

People are screaming
Someone call the police
I heard this sound, in disbelief

I wondered what that means
Too young to understand
Something went wrong
In fear they all ran

Moments later it stopped
I was carried down stairs
I see him in handcuffs
With an insane stare

I don't remember much
But that falling glass sound
I was only 2 years old
Looking up from the ground

I grew up, where this became normal
I may have lived, around the corner from you!

Play it Again

I replay that scene
A million times

The one shot in the chest
Who never hit the ground?
He turned and ran, with his sister in one hand
He was shot and bleeding; by a black man

The moment had slowed
Everyone was silenced
Things were moving in a blur of violence

The crowd just watched
There's a cop on the scene
My uncle was shot and I never heard a thing

I was standing in the front
With my bat in hand
I wanted to go and kill that man

He shot my uncle but didn't get away
His judgment would come; another day

That day was long
I remember it well
On the streets of Buffalo
A few blocks from hell

Shot in the chest
With a 12 gauge
Man oh man
I'll never forget that day

Hey Kid

Nine years old and
Trying to get away
Living life as a kid
In an unwanted place

I wanted to go home
But my father said no
So, the behavior of an idiot
Consumed my flow

I tried everything
To break this bond
But he wouldn't let go
And I needed my mom

He would not accept
That failed attempt
To make things better
In a life without him

More pain, than havoc
More sorrow, than joy
More bad than good
I was a good boy

In a life worth saving
I have counted my blessings
Blessed to have met him
But he never got the message.

Cut Down

As the sound of the sirens roar nears
I can hear them coming
As precious minute's slip away
The blood of a boy has reached the earth

His final moment captured by the moon light
This neighborhood has taken so many
With a single wound it seems life is transforming
As he looks up from the ground, I can see his fear

The fear of the unknown
Will this sidewalk be the last thing he sees?
Motionless, lying on the pavement
Am I witnessing the last moments of his life?

Sad and true the young women screams
She screamed "I didn't know they were going to do that"
Held back by the crowd she is defenseless
Crying and hysterical they pull her away

The blue and white cars arrive
They set boundaries for the on-lookers.
As rescue services try to save this boy
The shock of the situation is overwhelming

Now walking back to my block, I can't help but remember
Remember the times when that was almost me
Caught in the crossfire of confusion and rage
I escaped the nameless bullets
Cut down in the youth of his life
I can only wonder what the future holds for the rest of us
Will the cycles of drug abuse and envy, peek or subside?
or will our destiny or our self-destruction persist.

Mierda Eres Tu!

For that very first second
You were all I could dream
The creator's, creation
Giving life to the team

A flaw, never seen!

Iniquitous in a dream!

The taxing of a spirit!
Condemned to even live it!

Trick after Trick
And Chic after Chic

The absence of light
Is where this exists

The lies of chaos!

I must have lost it in a rhyme!

But I could never lose something!
That wasn't ever mine!

Now free from the shadows
Now released, to just breathe!

A reflection of secrets
From the mirror of deeds

As we reap, shall we sow
Is how that reads!

I put knowledge in the wisdom
Then grew it from a seed!

The Man in The Mirror

Memories in the light
Are terrifyingly bright

He gave us these moments
Living through these nights

In the days not forgotten
In the lives forever changed

A new peace has fallen
In the drops of the rain

As he stands in the mirror
Reflecting through time

Admiring his reflection
Perfection in his eye's

The mirror tells the story
How he does this all the time

The neighbors just listen
Because he yells all the time

Cursing at his image
Angry with time

Tormented by life
And the memories of a life time

Every second it gets worse
Not healthy for the mind

So, for the very first time
I asked him why

He had one reason
He said it was all in his mind

This was hard to accept
It had no logic or design

Just random outburst
His own image to curse

I could not understand
Where this all began

A single moment in time
In the seed of a mind

In the absence of truth
This seed grew without roots

Born into chaos

Fatherless in time

The saddest words ever written
By a son in a rhyme

He never had a chance
My example of a man

This world is unforgiving
But I have to keep living

He's "The Man in The Mirror"
"Freddy Man" to us all

Now the father becomes the son
With the father of us all.

Chapter 2

Is this Love?

Chapter 2 "Is this Love?" is my quandary. Is this my hopes and dreams? Is this what could have been?

"I was shattered not broken"

-Red Man

Love of Mine

Yes, they were romantic whispers!
They flowed through airs of life filled dreams
Carrying cascading images of great love and pain.

As I looked at her, my purpose appeared!

Visions of pride and life flowed in clouds of bliss

You see, I know she's here to complete my life and balance my fears

You see, God has sent her to me!

I am the man of a love so divine
Brilliant stars shy away!

I will capture the essence of love!

I will love harder than paper rocks!

You see, life before her never had sound

Before her, the sun was not as bright
I can still remember days of limitless growth

Back from the dawn of tomorrow
Devoted to loyalty and sacrifice
I will love her harder than your imagination

Beyond the realm of emotions and time
I will fill her soul with "Love of Mine"

Ms. Thing

She is smooth and wet, with the softness of life's most precious of
flowers.
As the taste of her flesh pulses against my desires, will I indulge myself in
the fruit of her virtue?

Can I caress and squeeze the bosom of her existence?
Or will she succumb to the overwhelming feelings of elation and ecstasy,
as I gasp for the words to describe the most penetrating of thoughts.

In her space!

Were these stolen moments the true face of our attraction?

Were they the conclusions of feelings, out of control?

Or will I wake up tomorrow and regret the taste of her?

Sidelines by the absence of raw emotion and logic, I still long for her
touch.

I can't get enough of her desires!

Pacing back through the mirrored images of our first physical encounter
I often pass the lost chances of time.

But still, with every breath of my being,
I still reach out for her.

For just moments of long-lasting gazes or seconds of intimate whispers.
The pursuit of this love illuminates my desires.

Caught in the moisture of her physical bliss, I can't help but indulge my
blessing into the juices of her voluptuous body. As I fondle the erotic
places between her mind and mine the sweat of our interaction is visible.
Strokes of this compounded energy has brought calm and clarity to a
moment filled with passion.

Will I reach the peak of her insatiable appetite or will she engulf the
essence of my existence before life gets in the way?

After all, has been said and done in this rhyme, the truth of the matter, is
that it is our time, so now I can say no matter what, that she is my truth
and "Super Juicy" to the touch,
I live to love her" for ever more, she is my Love, for whom I adore

Ready or Not

Soft and sweet
Curvy and loose
Perfection in motion
Is she, my truth?

Will she ignite my passion?
Or is she just a single flame?
Her eyes tell me yes.
But my heart is not the same.

I anticipate her touch
I dreamed of her smile
I wait for that moment
When she'll give me what's mine!

At first glance!
I was truly surprised!
I didn't expect that face
Or those beautiful eyes

I love that confidence
That she exudes so well
I can see her perfectly
She is that real!

She is that light
That I need in this life
I wish for the wisdom
To shine that bright

After all these lessons
In this life of mine
I wasn't ready for her
But I will be next time!

I've Got Nothin

If ever love has tested me, it has today
While standing on the plain of oblivion
I can see my world falling from the heavens

I can only find fragments of love and heartache,
in the space, in my chest

I've been reaching for that love, that was mine

I'm trying to put together that which I have lost
That in which I loved the most

I know, I'll never find all the pieces
But love will not get away

I will dig deeper than the deepest sea
I will climb higher than the highest mountain
To reach the love that killed my world

Will life prepare me for this journey?
Will the path of love show me the way?
Because I have to have this love, to live another day

Secret Data

Through the eyes of an angel
I reflect in time

She is the energy of life
The **G**reatest **O**f **A**ll **T**ime

She gave purpose to my vision
She is perfection in the vibe

On the frequency she designed
She adds beauty to the rhyme

She is Brittney! As "Bad Gets"!
She is knowledge, with assets!

She gave me words for the vine
To create magic on the lines

This is strange to the mind

We shared only minutes, in the vibe

But those seconds were divine
This is destiny in real time

I had to write it, in a wish
She is the chocolate that I miss

Now, I'll add it to the book
For inspiration and looks

I put my soul on the line
For seconds of her time

Now, I must rewind "All-Time"
She is the peace, I couldn't find!
She inspired these lines
She is my secret in the vibe

The Promise of You

I have been waiting for you
To meet me here
The promise of you
Has made life so clear

The thought of us
Has me smiling, yet alone
The thought of this love
Is beauty, I've never known!

The Beautiful You!!!
Has touched my heart
The need for this love
Has captured us apart

The comfort of finding
What I've lost
Has humbled my spirit
But at what cost

Will we cast these dreams?
Into a life time of chance
Or will we enjoy these moments
Filled with romance

I often wonder
What I would do
I have always been searching
For the promise of you

We are forever linked!
Forever in a rhyme
It's my desire for you
Forever in time!

The promise of you!
Has brought me here
The love in that promise
I want to share!

B. Marie

Two is just right
Two every night
Two lips in a dream
Four sets can be seen

The smell of your smile
Is driving me wild
The taste of her lips
Are in our first kiss

Is this your song?
I'd love to play along
I can fit in this place
And taste the smile on your face

We can talk and carry on
We can walk, in this song
We can live without lies
We can forever be tied

If this dream is alive
I can feel you in the vibe
I have craved your space
Since, I seen your face

I'm a lay this right here
So, I can be clear
The balance of a man
Is in the respect he demands

The love in his truth
He leaves up to you

In the absence of light
You are his sunshine

He knows the path to you
Is forever lost in time

The Dream

She was testing her limits
She put her soul on the line
She asked me for a minute
But I refused every time

I wanted that smile
The curve in her waist
I wanted to go deeper
Actually, live in her space

I wish she had known
That we shared the same dream
I could not tell her then
But I dreamed the same dream

I could see her moving
Up and down on the vine
She was with me in rhythm
Putting pressure on the rhyme

Pure sweat and emotion
I saw me in her eye's
I could smell the beginning
Of us enjoying the first ride

I pushed deeper by the minute
I was crushing seconds of her time

But the dream ended quickly
I was covered with the vibe

We dreamed the same dream
In the Plaza of secrets
She has the eyes of an angel
I wish you could see it.

Cy. Moore

Put it in the air!
I wanna vibe for a while

I want you here with me
Until the cypher comes alive

I love that walk
I watch it all the time

The curve of perfection

Brings softness to the vibe

A squeeze away from heaven

A moment away from time

In the presence of bliss
Her temperature begins to rise

She's hotter every second
She's touching all the lines

If that spot gets any hotter
It's will drip on the rhyme

Now her face is all flush

As she puts pressure on the vine

So, she blew it in the air
So, I could capture it on the lines

Now the words are all silly

They keep falling off the side

They're in love with this vision
Of her walking through time!

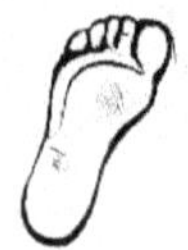
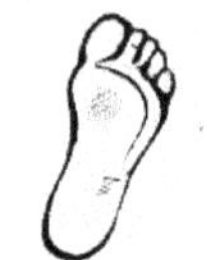

Loved

I've found you at last
I've come along way
From the City and beyond
To this present day

Now, I feel much better
Actually, kind of glad
That a love once lost
Has come back at last

You make me blush!
With that look in your eye

You'll make me complete
When you're by my side

Many years have past
And you still ignite that flame

The cross roads in life
Deserves no one to blame

The touching of one's heart
Is the true test of time?
I'm blessed to have known you
A new chance or a sign?

Dream'n

Life worth living
What a beautiful sound
The need for love spins me round

I wish for love
A wish in time
I can't stop hoping you will be mine

Places to go in this life of mine
I wait for that day; at a certain time
When I can look back and see your face
And dream of the time we were at this place

The stars had shined, on us that night
Love so solid, so fresh and right
I pledge my life and oh yes, my best
With this love, one dare not mess

Together at last, with my flow
Together in life, away we go
Reaching for stars, in this life of ours
Never standing still, it feels so real

I can't stop dream'n, of you right now
All I see, is good life and time
'

Will I awake, to a lonely room?
Am I destine, to be alone so soon?
Here it comes that awful sound
It's only the alarm, still going round

The Rainy Day

It's raining outside!
And all I can think of is you
Will the rain rinse away my desires?
Can it wash away the fondness of you?

The rain droplets beating across my window
Are casting images of your laughter and smile!
They also bring feelings of hope and progress
To a situation, uncertain and in rewind
The truth of life has capture us apart
But spiritually forever intertwined

Can we explore the feeling of today?
Without disturbing tomorrow

Is it a version of the truth that keeps us apart?
I wonder what the future holds

I dare not walk the road of misfortune
I have traveled this road before

When I think of us, I begin to smile
I can sense an attraction
No, I'm not in denial….
It's pressing and hot, not to be denied

It's a sign of affection
That I carry through time

Will we ever be alone?
I anticipate that day
I'll meet you anywhere
If you meet me half way.

Chocolate Cake

Served on Crystal
My favorite flavor on a plate

It comes in many layers

I want a slice everyday

I want to taste it daily
Maybe add strawberries and cherries

I told her as much
She has the filling that I lust

I bet it taste like chocolate
Chocolate Cake in fact

Always round on the bottom
Even thicker in the back

Creamier than the rest
I pick hers, as the best

With the one finger test
Every slice, I make a mess

This proves, I can't wait
It's like chocolate, check mate

Every drop of her cream
I can lick her lips clean

Any time of the day
I can eat the whole cake

I love chocolate cake
To end the first date.

That Girl

I have to smile
When I sit on her bed
I have to wonder
Will I make her turn red?

Will she look in my eyes?
Will she act really surprised?
Will she get undressed?
So, I can see her best

I want that girl
I want her real bad
I never wanted something, so much
That I already had

She feels so right
I long for that night
To get close again
It's hard to hold in

A beautiful smile
That gentle touch

I long for those things
I need her so much

Harry

I found this place
For us, to just vibe

The perfect page in space
To bring memories alive

In the year of the Rose
We partied all the time

Loving life to the fullest
Getting lost in the vibes

A Bishop and a Queen
The taste of my dreams

In the sounds of forever
No one could do it better

In the passion of those moments
We enjoyed the same ride

Being young and having fun
Our attraction was alive

I wrote this for you
So, you can read it anytime

It's my love for you
Traveling through time

If you remember this place
There is a smile on your face

If we ever meet again
I'll never let it end!

You

Planning this life
With only you in mind

Adoring your smile
And cherishing our time

You are so beautiful
A lady at all times

When I seen you walk
You inspired this rhyme

You move so well
And I love that strut
Will you meet me half way?
Or is that asking too much?

With that dark hair
And those beautiful eyes
I want to touch you!
It's no surprise?

What I wouldn't do!
For some time with you
I guess we'll never know.
In different directions we go.

I'll hope for better days
When we'll see each other again!
I miss seeing you smile
Forever your friend!

Caution

If I fell for you
Would you help me up?
Could you be that shoulder?
Instead of that crutch

Do we explore this place?
Or just imagine it in time
Shall I move a step closer?
So, we can complete this rhyme?

I'll take, two steps back
If you walk into my arms
I'll kiss every inch
If you have enough time

You are the forbidden
I know it's not mine
If you feel the same way
Please share in your design

With thoughts of benevolence
That I've cherished over time
I wrote this today
For a woman that's not mine

More

More and More
Is what I desire
The face of an angel
Fuels my fire…

Hot and Steamy
Yes, it's true
These images of lust
Have become my truth

It's in my being
To take moments in time
If I kissed your lips
Would you dare kiss mine?

I need to feed my soul
With you and your design
I'm waiting to touch your body
Forever wishing, it was mine

I'll count the seconds
Until I see you again
These are wishes in time
About time well spent

It's unimaginable
That we are forever linked, in a rhyme
It's beyond my control
That I can feel so inclined

If my thoughts had life
I could feel you right now
I could smell your essence
And taste your smile

Chapter 3
The Poet's Playground

Chapter 3 "The Poet's Playground" is where it all started. A fresh page and my pen!

"I make art with words"

-Red Man

Beef in a Rhyme!

It's a miracle I'm still standing
I just caught beef in a rhyme

I was articulating my affliction
When this gang of words dropped by

At last, I could see them.
They were corresponding in tone
They've been regrouping forever
Unable to achieve, rhythmic tone

So, one word at a time,
I lay in wait for a new rhyme
To admonish them again
As I rhyme about them

Knowledge of Self
As I stood on the first word
Introspection is wealth
As I illuminate their terms

I must carter these words
One rhythmic expression at a time
So they can lavish in their illusion
Like blemishes in time

How dare they step fast!
And no less, step on my page
With no reason or warning
No purpose to engage

This vexes me so
An enigma to the flow

I'm going to define their existence
With the eloquence of this revision

Divinely meticulous
As I navigate their terms
Slashing them to fragments
Punctuating their verbs

They're symbolic anecdotes

In literal form, with no design
I've been slapping them with rhythm
But, their unaffected by its design

So now, I'll take time
To break them down, in a rhyme
Then I'll decapitate them again
Because I'm still rhyming about them

I've manifested my focus
To create a rhyme, they would notice
But yet again, I can see them
Searching for truth, with no reason

But they're lost in translation
Because the words aren't patient

Now I'll remove them from time
One vision into one mind
"The Path of Enlightenment"
"The Articulation of a Rhyme"!

I can change these words
Change them all around in time
So you can remember what you heard
It's the path of my design

I used these words
As an example of a paradigm
To show you the blue print
Of how to phonetically explain "Why"

I had to transformed their meaning
Into phrases worth seeing
I had to inject more wisdom
To create words to envision

This led to more rhythm
The revolution of more rhymes
The pinnacle of my aspirations!
From catching "Beef in a Rhyme"

My Pen

I haven't touched her yet
She knows I'm outside
I use her to write
She connects words to the vibe

This page is all wet!
She spilled a verse on the lines
It was dripping with knowledge
I saw wisdom in the rhyme

The words were so sexy
I was sliding between the lines
I had to hold on, to the page
Until she skipped another line

Her tips are so curvy
She is sharper than you and I.

She placed a word on the image
The image began to shine
The shine began to flow
The flow landed back on the lines

It is hard to admit
That "My Pen" is alive
She's the lyrical mastermind
That I carry through time

Her hustle is so sick
She put magic in my wrist
She cast spells in the lyrics
Just so I can hear it
Now the page is alive
This is poetry that's mine

I am the owner of the vibe!
She's "My Pen" that's alive.

Trapped

I've seen this place
I've been here before
It smells of you
I can't take it anymore

Where are you now
I want to see your face
I'm in here again
In your space

Is this a trick?
Let me know
I want to get out
Let me go

I've tried every door
I've searched every room
I always end up here
Back in this poem

I'm tired of searching
I wish this would end
I'm trapped in this dream
That will never end

Alkebulan

A creation of dignity, stolen from history

"The Mother of Mankind", removed from the timeline

In the "Garden of Eden", lived knowledge and freedom

In the glory of existence, they shared wisdom and riches

Then the plot, of his plans
Changed the color of a man!

The European invasion of the mother land

A truth never told, wiped from the globe

The colonizing of minds spread over centuries by design

The colonizers, colonizing, the land before time

Then time was reset
From zero in rewind

The first steps of his truth, justified by lies

Now dynasties and kingdoms, are separated by lines

First divided then conquered, then robbed over time

The truth of his origin, is why his hatred would rise

He was enlightened by the Moors and educated by the times

But the "Knowledge of Self" could not penetrate his mind

So, I had to illuminate these words on the lines!

So, the light in the wisdom
Could be seen in your eye's!

On the Way

I can't see
Turn on the lights
I've been in here a while
Is it night?

Lots of water
Lots of mush
I keep wondering
What is this stuff?

I can hear voices
They're all muffled and rough
I want to get out
Moving is tough

Hold that thought
I feel a push
My heads all wet
I feel a rush

Are those hands?
What could that be?
Surprise, surprise
It's just me!

Alive

At last, the night has come
And as the moon rises over the clouds
The hood is alive
Alive with the hustle of life

Chasing that Jones
Ready for what ever
Inspiring and dangerous
Never asking any question

I love my hood
It's the place of dreams
It keeps me on point
Keeps my eye on things

With effortless flows
Through faces of denial
It's the essence of confusion
With no way out

Compounded with violence
With enough opinions to go round
I see gaps in this future
It's not hard to figure out

Does my future shine bright?
Or am I forever lost in the night
I've lived here forever
Looking forward into the light

Many have come, to play this game
Never briefed on the street, they pulled up lame
I've captured my block, every trap, every gap
If you see me scrambling
Do me a favor ---HOLLA BACK.

Age & Wisdom

The age of time
Often comes with wisdom
The privileges of life
Often have their restrictions

Despite these misfortunes
Many would call them sublime
I travel the world plenty
Ever abreast of its design

The philosophical anecdotes
Ever ready but benign
Bring visions of benevolence
From the Earth in decline

With a thirst for intelligence
And an aptitude for intellect
Shall I reach for the dialect?
That has made this poem so eloquent

With ever verse more intricate
More convoluted over time
I've partaken in its malfeasants
However illicit in design

The path of this wisdom
Blessed with age over time
Brings a life of privilege
Which I created in a rhyme

Motherless Child

Not forgotten but still alone
She sleeps in a bed that's not her own

Placed in a foster home where no one cares
Sent there to live with five other kids

Where is my mother?
She often asks
Where's my family?
The other kids just laughed

Lost in the system
With no one that cares
A life with no mother
What a burden to bear.

Her life is so empty
She often doubts herself
She even questions her existence
She has no knowledge of self

This child needs love
That only a mother can give
She made a promise to God
Never to abandon her kids

Poetry

This kid just asked me
Why I write these poems
I explained to that kid
That poetry is a zone

It's a space to feel free
A place to walk alone
It's that space to live dreams
Through the words of a poem

It's a poetic journey!
I'll take you on a trip
To the moon and beyond
Pass stars we can split

Phenomenally lyrical
Astrological with the flow
Futuristically rising
Through the clouds like snow

I rock in all seasons
Always, like time
I wait for no man
To try his words against mine

Standing on the earth
For just seconds in time
I graduated from life
With a masters in design

The design of rewind
Is spinning out of control
I'll end this little journey
With a poetic outro

I've been blended in time
And squeezed from fresh air
I'm giving you the future
You should take it and share

It is, What it is!

It is, what it is!
Is about living life with no shame

It is! What it is!
Is about truth with no blame

It's like
Living, life with no guide
It's like
Ready to go, with no ride

It's like
Being hungry with no food
It's like
Being ugly and still rude

It's like
Drunk for no reason
It's like
High all the time

It's like
Homeless doesn't matter
It's like
Life undefined

It's like
These things don't matter
No matter time or place

This is the way life is
Because
It is, What it is!

Useless

I seen you out there
Just wasting away
You look so hungry
Can I loan you a day?

This day is for rest
It's always on time
Can you stay for a minute?
I want to explain this rhyme?

One day among many
A time to check self
Am I doing me any good?
I need to ask myself

No one cares
That I'm on my own
I can still hear your voice
"This is your life in this poem"

No wonder I left
It's too hard to do right
The days are too long
And it's easier to do wrong

With both eyes open
I choose to live here
This is my life!
There are no rules over here

Banter

A cosmic snapshot
Into a mind and a rhyme
It's the path of wisdom
That I travel on through time

With the knowledge of self
I write verse after verse
Blending wisdom and words
Into a vision of self

I usually stretch these verses!

Mold them to the rhyme
The mastery of the vibe
Proves the flow is alive

I re-rolled it and lit it
I began to hear voices and lyrics

I feel so alive
I think the flow, got me high

I can put you in the mix
With this pen, Boy I am Sick

With the patience of the vibe
I can point at you with the rhyme

I had set fire to the lyrics
Just so you can hear it

This page is burning too quick!
Damn that can't be it!

Covid

In the damn house!!
This sh%ts gotta stop!
The world is infected!
Believe it or not!

I just put my mask on
And quietly breeze out!
These cone heads be trippin
"The Pink Toe of Doubt"!

You can "Live or Die"
The President said
He's the 45th disaster
On this stolen land

The Proud Boys are coming
I'm waiting every night
Bigots with guns
That can't even fight

If I catch you around here
Ill chop off ya lyrics

Then I'm a pack you in a spliff!
Because I only smoke the real sh%t!

That's the world I'm in
Everyday I'm locked in
I need to get out
I'm worse in the south
I'm worse than you can imagine
In my circle, I'm the savage

I'm just blasting through walls
Trying to find these fools
But they movin like roaches
Ducking in the grooves

I want them to know
That as far, as I go
I wish a mothaf#&ka would
Now you'll stay Hood!

One Way or Another

I've battled the bottle
I've smoked all night
I've failed at work
Your misery's my life

To wake up sober
Feels unreal
I wish it would end
I'm yours to kill

Times too slow
I'm wasting away
I'll have another drink
While you're on your way

Will you take me fast?
Will I have to live on?
Will you spare me pain?
Are you leading me on?

I want to die
What's your deal?
Do want me to do it
I swear I will

My time has come
It's your move now
Take me quick
Or I'll show you how

Hungry

I'm starving mad
With hunger pains
No food to eat
And no one to blame

It's a hard knock life
When you live so trife
It's not hard to tell
When you've tried and failed

It's hard to stand tall
When you don't give it your all
But I'll be that crutch
If it matters that much

I'll feed all four
With four bucks
I've done it before
We never had much

I'll stretch the sky to feed what's mine
I'll bend those rules
If we have no food
I'll never give up
Until we've had enough!

There are nights I've cried
But we've made it through
I'll do what it takes
Just for you!

The Essence of Life

I am Family

I'll help you in a jam
I'll be that extra hand
I am the essence of you
Do you know who I am?

The essence of life
Can only mean one thing
The strength of family
The courage we bring

From day one, we are taught one thing
To protect what's, ours or don't come in
Family is the essence, of this life of mine
Without my family, I could not shine

The love I feel, when we're having fun
Makes life so clear, it's like the sun
It's something I need to stay alive
It's something that's necessary in my life

The essence of Life
Is not a dream
It's the gift of family
It means everything!

I feel the pain

The pain of life
The pain in your name
I feel that pain, one in the same
I am Junior
Hear me now

I've lived this life
Without a guide
The pain of living
It's called abuse
It's too late to help
You've been no use

The pain in my name
Has come from you
I try to understand, what did you do
Where were you, when I grew up!
Where were you, when times got tough!

I can't find a way
To relieve that pain
I write this now to understand your game
To my nephew Kilo, I feel that pain
We share that pain, one in the same

In spite of chance
You must complete this dance
I know it's hard, this life of ours
I feel that pain, that's in your name
Where's my Dad? he's the one to blame

The Walk

I'm re-walking the walk
To my end
Shot down in the street
By my friend

Never saw it coming
Never could have thought
That money and drugs
Would complete this thought

I see me dying
Bloody as hell
One shot to the dome
Clutching my scale

I need some help!
I need some space!
It's not my time
To leave this place.

Flow

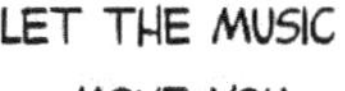

A thinking man's folly
Clever word play, on the lines
With this wheel, we roll
Up and down the timeline

Catching verbs at play!
Watching vibes come alive!
With these lyrical vibrations!

The rhythm

Begins

To rise!

It sounds like cleverness!
Can you really get loose with the rhyme?

Wait?

What?

Hold This!

I roll up well and I got my eyes on the loot
With that fat ass booty, she jumped out of the coup

I got rides outside
In the different color blue's

Can you feel that beat?
I'm about, to bus a move

The pen and the pad had to stay in the room
This is "Red Man" Mobbing
Straight for you

It started as freestyle

When I got the mic

But they challenged
"The God"
To a lyrical street fight

So, I crushed his lyrics
Reconstructed his vibe

Then smacked him with the rhythm
Then asked him why
Do you live this way?

What's "The God" to say?

I just ride with these lyrics
One day at a time

Just chopping through vibes
Until the page comes alive

I pardon these fools

They know not!
"The Rhyme"

If I added another verse
I would be wasting my time!

Little Man

Why would you live by the gun?
If you're only gonna run
Why would you move to my hood?
If you're up to no good

I ask these questions
To understand your design
I'm astute and ready
To watch your decline

You have no clue
What the hood will do
Will you take a step back?
Before the hood attack

I speak of fate
That life on the street
A hustle still flowing
Waiting to absorb the weak

If you know, like I know
You will bounce where you stand
You will take these warning
As advice for a young man

The hood is an animal
Always ready and undefined
Taking life without warning
From young men caught in time

I hope you're not scared
It's violence in this crowd
You look like the new jack
You better watch out

I Am Man

Positively masculine
Never to be confused
Overly boisterous
And not easily amused

A man among plenty
Many have no clue
What it takes to be a man
I may be referring to you

Could you teach that boy?
Could you show him the way?
Could you raise another man?
Without leading him astray

It's positively imperative
That we accomplish our goal
To lead these men
Into a better World!

I have my own
Santana's my son
I'll teach him well
Until the end of my run

He is my mission
I'll show him the way
To be strong and proud
The Native Way!

Life

This life of mine
I wonder its meaning
It moves so fast
I'm wondering if you've seen me

I play real hard
I maximize my time
I take many chances
I'm having a good time

When I enjoy this life
It feels so grand
To have one regret
Would disappoint this man

A man among many
A man among men
For the ladies to enjoy me
Is a life well spent?

I have conquered my fears
I have taken that chance
I have lost love once
But I've found it again

I must take that love
And hold it tight
Never to lose it
Without a fight

My heart I pledge
In this life of mine
It's all I have
Until the next time

Hope

To the clouds in heaven
To the Great Spirit up above
Can you give me the strength?
Can you show me some love?

I've traveled this earth
During this life time
I've seen only havoc
And misspent time

My journey is unclear
Many have lost their way
The footprints of man
Have led me astray

For this world to flourish
We must grasp this rhyme
We must change man's direction
Before he destroys our time

The goal is set forth
Crystal and Clear
For this time to continue
We must love, not fear!

Destiny

Whispers in the dark
The moan of fear
Back from the dead
With no grudge to bear

I have come for you
That darkened swine
The worst of man
The only one of his kind

The bottom feeder
That lost child
The one who doesn't care
That lives to tell lies

Can you be redeemed?
Is there light on your side?
Are you destine for forgiveness?
Just this one time

I don't think so
You have nowhere to go
I'll give you a ride
I'm at your side

To the depths of hell
Where our destiny awaits
I've brought you here
Because you love to hate.

True Friend

I seen you today
It's been a while
I mentioned what I wrote
I wanted to see you smile

My private thoughts

With you in mind
You're all I need
To complete this rhyme

I think of you often
Like a friend of course
I hope it's not creepy
There only word in a verse

It's hard to believe
You have entered my book
Through poetry and intrigue
That's off the hook

Being your friend
Is all it is?

Seeing you smile

Making you laugh

Wanting to hold your hand
Because, friendship lasts

Time will tell
If it means that much
A wish in time
It's no rush

A friend in time
Plus me, equals us
All I wish
Is to make you blush

I Get It...Now!

I've been honest with you
I expect the same
The mess I'm in
There's only me to blame

If you have an issue
You should have let me know
I have no time to play
I can play with my flow

What you've done
I've done to others?
I think it's cute
I'm not even bothered

To be coy and vague
To be out of sight and out of mind
To be missing for days is truly not a crime
I've done these things

I've led them astray
It was my choice, to play this way

Player; play on; I detect good game
For me to hold on would be a damn shame

I've played real hard, I've said too much
I think I'm to close; I can still feel your touch

I wish for truth, just to satisfy that urge
I don't expect a response; not even a word

Blonde

Is it blonde?
Is it really!
Can I see?
Is it merely!
A small patch
Or a run way strip.
Or maybe a bush, that I could not miss.
I wonder what.
I want to see.
I bet its breath taking
and all for me.

Fairy Tales

Wake up fast
That's not me
A dream so wet
What could that be?

Where is that place?
You play so well
I want to watch
I will not tell

It sounds so hot
It smells so real
Play with my flow
While time stands still

Can I feel you move?
Will you play with mine?
Can I move in this dream?
If it's not mine

A dream so wet
A dream of me
Wish me there
So I can see

Tremble

I can feel you tremble
The heat is intense
I feel you panting
I'm filled with suspense

When I kiss your lips
I tremble with desire
When I touch that spot
Does it get any hotter?

Can we go real slow?
Can I take my time?
I love your tremble
It's so divine

Do you care that much?
Is it really that good?
The way you tremble
Makes me feel so good

The search for that kiss
Makes me wish
That a women like you
Could make me tremble too!

Can't Move On

Why did we meet?
What was the purpose?
My hearts been broken
I've lost my focus

What do you want?
Is it me!
I want you so much
I wish you could see

That time is gone
It makes me sad
That a love so strong
Could turn so fast

It drives me crazy
Wondering oh maybe
What could have been?
If you had let me in

That time spent; was a Blessing
I'd do it again with no question
A fool for love is who I am
To search for you is my plan

Signed
"The Fool"

Never Forget

I've found that place
That place in my heart
Without you there
It seems time has stopped

The need for love, has run aground
The sound of your laughter
No longer has sound
I feel for you, like no other
The thought of you, is no bother

The dream of us, has faded away
I only hope, to relive that day
Time in this space
It feels like a waste
I have no regrets, in this case

I wish you success
In whatever you do
I'll never forget, the loss of you
Life goes on, in every space
Never forget about this place

Thinking of You

Sitting and waiting for that time to come
Hoping and thinking about the end of our run
I disguise my distaste with a grin on my face
I regret this mess but I gave it my best

I have much to say
I'm thinking of the best way
To express myself, without your help

I've found many words
Many nouns, many verbs
But what I can't figure out
Is how it went south?

Was it too many nights, was it too many fights?
Was it a bad touch that meant too much?

I wonder what, I think of it often
It consumes my thoughts
The thought of you, is often

Times must change
I know it must
But when I try to forget
I can't help but cuss

I'm reminded of you, and thinking of us
I miss that friendship, I miss it.......much
I can't stop writing, you motivate my soul
Life without you, feels so cold

Mine

Traveling the world
Moving in time
It's my only dreams
That you'll never find

My secret place
Where only the sun shine's
The end of the world
Where there's only me and time

My minds wide open
Waiting for you to appear
I've been waiting forever
It's for you that I live

With oceans of fun
And a lifetime of bliss
With you at my side
How could I miss?

I'm waiting for love
In my sacred place
I pray you'll come
And take your place

Day One

In the beginning there was melanin!
Brown skin in the sunshine

The only people on earth
In the beginning of mankind

She was "Eve" in creation
The first woman on the timeline

The proof of her existence
Is in the code of our blood line

The truth in every man
Lies the seed of the land

The elevation of creation
Began in this nation

The mastery of the land
The cleansing of the mind

The history of humans
Documented through time

From here we began
Giving life to the land

In all directions of the globe
Every "Race" would unfold

The source of this knowledge
Is now unlocked on the lines

A plethora of wisdom
Foretold as a sign

Wishes

If I met you in the future
Will you show me the past?
If I know what is coming
Do you think it will last?

Can you promise me new life?
Beyond this place
Can you grant me one wish?
Maybe two in this case

The first is what's needed
To capture you, in time
To be hopelessly in love
Until the end of this rhyme

The second is so smooth
I want to be that dude
I want to dwell in your space
And put a smile on your face

Time

The wish of time
A wish un-answered
A mere thought in time
I have no answers

I've waited so long
I've played my part
It's not my fault
This has turned so dark

I'll look for you
In the open air
I'll long for you
The future's unfair

Time to part
It's never the end
Time to move on
Always as friends

The pleasure was mine
I enjoyed your space
In time we'll look back; on this place
The memory of you, shines so bright
I'll never forget that first night!

The Hat

"The Hat" is in my room

Comedian or pure fool?

The laughing never stops
Prank Calls and ease drops

Joanna in the Dukes
Scared "The Hat" with one look

The funniest sh%t I ever saw
She said "come here"
He said "naw"

He surfaced a little later
He said, "I trust you, most of all"

He wanted to smoke his first joint
With me in Lima Hall

I said "hell yeah"
I was running low, in fact

So, we put it in the air
Then he "threw up" after that

I was cussing and screaming
"You better clean this sh%t up!"

He just laid there for a while
Just laughing it up

So, I finished that spliff
Because he was done in 2 hits

He eventually came back
He said never again, after that

Now, I see him on TV
Starring on "Late Night"

Thirty years from the Rose
Still funny in real life!

I am the "Peace" my brotha!

The love I have for my children, my family and friends, is eternal. I understand you my Sista, with all your flaws and every perfection. I understand you my Brotha, because every color of man has his advantages and disadvantages in this world. I need all of you to hear this!

First, the world needs you to take care of yourself and everything you create. Take care of yourself at all times and do the right thing for yourself, not because that is what is expected of you, because it's the right thing to do for you!

Secondly, the world needs you to take care of your family. Take care of them, show them love, give them guidance. Give them what they need to become productive parts of society and humanity.

Thirdly, the world needs you to take care of your community. This is where you live and other families like you live. Take care of the life around you. Your community is where our future grows.

Lastly, we have to start taking care of one another no matter what color we are.

I am talking about human responsibility.

I am talking about righteousness

I am talking about right and wrong
I am talking about the path of God

"I am not obligated to feed my Brotha, but he is welcome to some of my portion"

-Red Man

This ideology of actually helping your fellow man is practically non-existent across this world. The world environment will not entertain the thought of this because economic conditions across the world are planned and organized. The people and organizations that do participate in these efforts are few and fall well short of making a significant impact.

Although we are different in appearance, culture and understanding we are all still human beings and we have a basic human responsibility to respect each other and contribute to our species.

I'm sure that this will be a wakeup call to those that have the burden of self-loathing and the irresponsible attitude of "I did not ask to be here". This is why the world is in this condition.

If religion is the center of your life, no matter what religion it is, then let this enhance your human experience on this earth. Do not let this lead you away from the "Human Responsibility" that you have to the life you have been blessed with.

Please excuse my directness, my words at times run free. We must be smarter and stay informed. You think what they show us on TV is real? Well, it's not; it's what they allow us to see. They are distracting us from what is really going on. They have organized our community so we have to pay them for their societal legal standards, that they have created. They call it federal and state government, free market capitalism and holidays; I call it "Perpetual Debt", it's really a trap to keep you under privileged and ignorant to the reality of modern society.

I appreciate you all so much that the vehicle in which I was trying to find to deliver you this message terrible vexed me. So, this is my path. I have to write it! My efforts are directed to expressing the principles of individual human responsibility in modern time, then moving forward! At least how I see it! I am a thinking man trying to be better for myself and my family. I love life! I love living life! I love "ME and You"! How about that!!!

This message is to inform you to take better care of yourself and your family. Society has turned us into people who care more about surviving and trying to stack paper then identifying the importance of taking care of and cherishing "Human Life".
The significance of what you do and how you do it, in reality demonstrates to the next generation that comes after you the importance of "Individual Human Responsibility."

Most will be intrigued as to why I am saying this. The truth of the matter is because at least one of you need to hear this. I know many will glance this over or read it without comprehending anything, so I have to document these ideas and information because it is my understanding and knowledge. Questioning my motives goes to show you how much we have all taken the time to understand "Purpose"!

Chapter 4
Introspection

Chapter 4 "Introspection" is my testimony

"The source of my motivation can be found in the words I choose to share"

-Red Man

Magic Jordan

Dear Mama's
My Pretty, Pretty
All that is good in me, I have given to you
I have made you stronger than I needed too

You will need this strength
To live with this love
I will not be here forever
But forever watching from above

You are that "Love" that I carry inside
Forever my heart, for all time
My life's joy is to see you smile
The Love of a Father, Blessed with Time

Time to teach and lead my seed
The A,B,C's and even to read
The thought of this love is stronger than me
I have tears for you that only I can see

I will always be there is spirit and heart
I will always be watching even in the dark

I will never waiver from your favor
I will never cry when you say goodbye
I will always care even in despair
I will always love from the heavens above

My hearts wide open for you to share
I've waited so long for you enter my air
I will always be there to the end of time
You are the gift of life, the essence of mine
Jordan, I LOVE YOU…Papi

By Design

Basking in time
As the sun approached
Indefatigably wondering
About the dream I wrote

In this dream
I wrote of the divine?
How we sat in the future
And conversed over time

He felt so real
His life so defined
He's the reason I live
He's love all the time

With ever thought by design
Even bad thoughts in rewind
He's the only one of his kind
It's the way of his design

He keeps me moving
In and out of his design
He made love into rhythm
So I put it into rhyme

The divine is everywhere
Both heaven and sunshine
It's the way he loves
It's his love by design

Auntie Na.

I can still see your smile!
I remember it so clear!

Beauty and intelligence
With a world of love to give
But, with this lifetime of memories
Only my tears can say goodbye

I know the pain has ended
I know you're in a better place
But I miss you so much
I think of you often throughout the day

Will time help my soul?
Will time prepare me for this life?
I never thought this would happen
I never imagined us apart

I can remember the times
When we laughed and we cried
I can remember the times
When your life touched mine

I have so many things to tell you
I wanted to show you my book
I've been writing about us
I can remember so much!

Tai-Nai Lee has a poem
Your nephew Kilo does too
My heart is so heavy
It's hard to write about you

I remember we talked about this book
Too put our family on the map
It's hard to imagine
But I'm doing just that
It's because I love you

That I had to write this poem
You're my favorite auntie
The best friend I've ever known.

My Creator

I woke up today
In the glory of his space

My vibration was high
As I entered his grace

As I walked his path
His light touched my face

He was giving me directions
With his eternal embrace

I live in his glory
He understands my ways
I pray to him daily
Anytime of the day

I pray for guidance
On a frequency he designed
We are always together
Sharing verbs on the lines

If his message is unclear
I just pray another time
Then I asked for forgiveness
For being lost in the rhyme

His path is my journey
It started with no guide
So, he opened my eyes
Now I stay at his side
He made me the energy
I am "Pure Love" on the lines
My place is beside him
He is your eternal lifeline.

Chapter 5
Slam Poetry

Chapter 5 "Slam Poetry" is a collection of performance pieces. The creativity in my imagination running wild!

"The smartest people listen more than they talk"

-Red Man

Circumstances

The circumstances of life have led me here, to blend mind and time, into words that appear.

Into many miles of imagination
I have captured the essence of smiles

Smiles are the cravings of alone!

You see, as a native man I have been to the interview where I will never be enough. I have been everything from a boy, to a man, to nothing and still I can stand here and tell you, my pain. With a chance at success, I may conquer the walls of the mistreated, with unmentioned rivers of homicidal genocide, complete with an ocean of hate and a million miles of lies and betrayal.

You see history has shown me the future of mistakes.

You see, where the lies are buried in the library is where the truth lies. I said "You see, where the lies are buried in the library is where the truth lies. If you want to find it, it's there.

Back in bounce, we have taken this information back to the lab to be dissected and interjected, we have ostracized it and magnified it with both mind and soul into flames of disagreements mixed with renditions of past war experiences which we have concluded as "False".

You see my people were here first! You can't discover people that were already here. This is crazy; you can't take an entire race of people and say you go live over there. What is that, the mistreatment of a Red Man in retreat, because the world of choice is no longer fair?

I have stood for this long enough. I will take masses of geographic plains into fields of dreams, upon heavenly bodies of time and decimate that which is "You"!

You will be subject to aromatic flows of wisdom and knowledge that will change the structure of your being.

I can conquer you!

In this plain of spiritual light the stars of smoke dancing warriors have descended onto the faces of colorless fear. An upright man filled with self-appointed ignorance to the inherent facts of civilization. I have come to show you the errors of his ways. I can show you the plan of design to incarcerate all that is mine. The files of raised hate and injustice that fills the walls of his soul, blocking the airs of freedom.

Through ill-gotten time the nourishment of the earth will unite with my being and change the aspirations of a mind in alignment. Aligned with the solar bodies of magnetic dreams I push past this turbulence and trial. I will fly past the chains of oppression and explode on the Earth as a Chief of the missing people of a land of freedom.

Yes, a missing people lost to the pages of time. The lost images of a society rich in pride and culture.

Yes, we will take back the overdeveloped lies of hatred and greed. There will be no more years of injustice or ill-gotten lands. The Raping of the Earth will come to an end. The tears of modern time lack the wisdom of freedom.

Through literal balance and poetic fields, my words resonate through the smoke-filled images of my ancestors.

Charged by the essence of existence The Great Mother Earth exists as a tool of spiritual freedom.

Leaping off the pages of history into modern time, I write to inform ignorance and change. Through pass discretions we arrive at the presents of truth. Always here but never seen.

I once told a colorless man, that I was "A Native American" and he said, "You don't look like a Native American". What does that mean? I don't look like the image of lies pasted down in your schools!
I am "Visible in Disguise"!

That's the world I live in.

Is it the response of ignorance to befriend, "alone"?
Is it the world of lines and borders that confuses our place in history? Is
this land my land, or the one who has paid his taxes? What actually can a
man own without the colorless man taking his claim?

Is the reservation the only safe place from the "absence of color"?

For clarity one must ride the emotions of time into a place of divine
freedom and understanding. Soar free into the landscape of the Great
Spirit and beyond. Grace images of prosperity and harvest, through gaps
of leisurely moving waters from the depths of the abyss.

I have arrived!

I have arrived from the flames of native voices, unheard and unseen.

I have arrived to right the wrongs of literal sound.

I have arrived from my four father's visions of sovereignty and
independence.

I have arrived!

Here I'll plant the seeds of pride and dignity, "The light of a people
illuminates through my existence". It speaks of the journey of Native
America and the invasion of the colorless man.

Astute and brazen young natives have armed themselves with the history
of his story. The facts of Native America and the decline of a world not
designed for the colorless man.

"Through higher levels of enlightenment coincided with depths of
character yet undefined", I can see him for who he is.

The wicked one!

Wicked in nature, disease overseas; lies of purged lives caught in a cycle
of a predetermined existence that could never be truly righteous.

Yes!

That is he!

He waits at the edge of life's eternal cliff, hoping for forgiveness for 500
years of tyranny, rape and murder.

Swallowed by ignorance, choking on its design. He has reached the
climax of his existence.

Aligned

As rays of sunlight reflect off the waters of the Atlantic, I am in alignment with my creator. I can speak freely of the time of misfortune. While walking through the velvet meadows of life's journey, I have stumbled over the truth. With images of prosperity and growth I have seen the rise of a people, forgotten and unafraid. Yes, unafraid of the colorless death. You see every treaty we have written has been broken. Both disrespected and holistically effected our lives carry on.

Pride and dignity is from where I have come. Enlightenment and his story is my future. For he has given me the knowledge to see him for who he is. Armed with ideas of betrayal, I cannot match his evil. I am not built to kill freedom. I am a man of native decent that smiles at the thought of his demise. From the time his boat landed in Jamestown my people have paid with their lives. Given all that this land has to offer, still he wants more. Mother Earth provides everything we need, we told him. But nothing is ever enough.

The creator has shown my people the ways of Turtle Island. Mother Earth provides all. We only take what we need from her. The greed of the colorless man is unmeasured. Blank faces of colorless lies have invaded the souls of the Native Americans. Assimilation is his tool of his domination. Can he retract a culture, rich in the bloom of human existence?

From here I will fight with the words of the unspoken. I will bring his-story to our young. The images of a culture in decline will be swept away by knowledge and fact. By the design of the creator our people will rise again. With the freedom to practice our way of life, language and culture, we will honor the creator with these gifts. Even though modern times have changed the faces of our people, still we remain strong in a land of freedom.

Both unseen and obscure the plight of Native Americans is ongoing in our nation highest courts. They have taken so much from us. The amount of lost life alone has determined his future. Although my voice speaks to the masses it is still not enough to unhand his grip. Now, I wait. I wait for the next young warrior to step forward into our destiny and fight his-story with his words on our stolen land.

Unstoppable Savage

As I move off the path of light, I am blinded by the looks of the devilishly inclined, nomads of ignorance and discord. While moving to the beat of the Great Spirit I see many of my people lost and alone. Killed off by the devils men. Kill off by his poisons and disease as we tried to retrieve that which was ours, but he brought loud booms and hot metals. This was the beginning of the end for my people. With pride they fought and died for this island and from the past I was sent from the eyes of the true people of Turtle Island. From here is where I have come with the Bravery and Strength of 1000 warriors and 2000 bows, with a thirst for knowledge that could block out the sun and a hunger for blood that would take years to swim through. But humbly I approach.

Slowed by the times of laws and privilege I have taken my place at the end of society. But please hold on, I can't wait any longer, the essence of a warrior has risen. Through the leather straps of my war club I will find the answers to the reasons. I will find the path of my people. I will see the steps that have brought our futures together. I have taken aim at the colorless faces of the world that have invaded my land and as they parish in time as the sun approaches, we will speak to the Great Spirit and determine the source of their wickedness. As ashes from the sky drop on small waters, I can feel the ways of my ancestors. Wise and experienced is the path of my ancestors. Many life lessons to pass down! But I have made my pact with the world and I am here right now and ready to take form.

I am the Unstoppable Savage.

The Unstoppable Savage is both man and verse
He's here to live, love and show the world his curse
The Unstoppable Savage is the essence of me?
It's not my name; it's who…I be!

I'll learn you something, I'll let you see
I just prepared this blessing for you, not me
Savage is what they call me but Unstoppable is what I seem to be

America's Truth, they don't know what to do with me
From the Reservation to the city over looked by many

From the east to the west, I've sought the best
Seneca by blood, come and see
You know where I live, you know where I be!

I was suppose to die, in my father's time
I was suppose to perish, from the devils marriage
I was suppose to hurt, when they raped mother earth
But now I'm found, 6'3 off the ground

I have no tears for all those years
I can't cry; you know why
I'm savage and free with an iron will
Only 85 hundred that you didn't kill

I will survive I will live on
You can't stop me, I'm the unstoppable one

"The gift of knowledge, I bestow in haste"
No one can stop me
No time to waste

Historically Savage! Native by birth
It's the name, they gave us, so I put it to verse

I am that savage
One paw and a rhyme
The spirit of life!
Turtle Island in design!

Savagely moving, unstoppable in time
A hustle still flowing, one line at a time
I wrote these words with you in mind
Putting one and two together with three at a time

My native status, my savage ways
My forgotten culture, the ancient days

It's the truth of life, unstoppable at times
Could I've made this up?
In an unstoppable rhyme

Savage overtones an unstoppable design
I put pin to paper who knew it would rhyme

Happiness through misery
I got mine before time
I took life for granted
I'm savage in rewind

I've never done that before
I know of the divine
He's forgiveness and love
He savage all the time

The unstoppable words
In an unstoppable rhyme

I'll bus a funky--dope move
That's savage in design

Today I'm here but tomorrow in rewind
The Unstoppable Savage the only one you'll find

I'll die on my feet
Before I live on my knees
I'll trade a good death
Before, I do him
A good deed

I'll never give up
Unstoppable you'll see
Savagely resurrecting
The unstoppable me

I've reached that point, that poetic zone
I feel words don't matter
It's just me in this poem

Can you walk in my path?
Can you step in my shoes?

Can you see the savagery?
We've been set up to lose!

Raise your head
Step back in time
Remember that verse
When I started this rhyme

"The gift of knowledge I bestow in haste"
No one can stop me
No time to waste

Now that you know
The truth is just that
Never fold for any one
Never fall back!

Unstoppable living
Is the only choice
To succeed at success
Do hear my voice?

My time has come
To put away this flow
I want you to hear this
Before I go

The thought of us
Has inspired others
One beautiful thought after another

I share with you
A piece of me
A love of life
That all can see

A poetic journey
A lyrical dream
If you be real quiet
You can hear everything

Final Quote

"I would never advise my children or any of my family members to ever quit anything that they started. I am not a quitter and I don't promote that in any form, but if anyone does decide to quit anything in their lives, I would only hope that they would choose to "Quit Being A Hater"

-Red Man

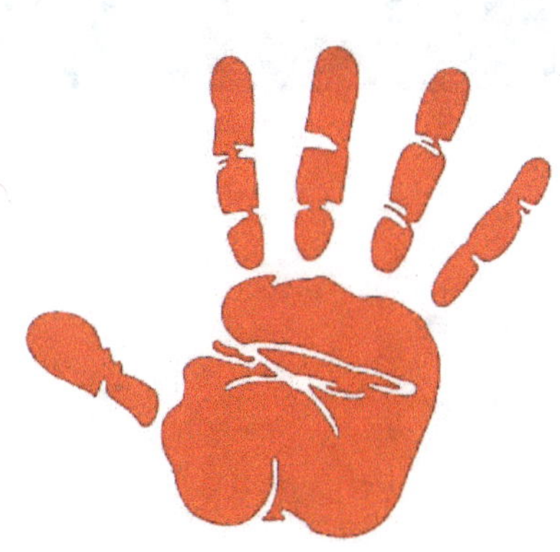

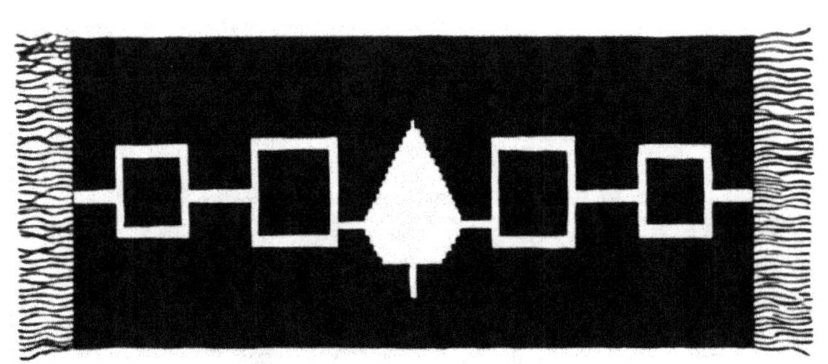